Thicket Monitoring at Homestead National Monument of America 2000 - 2010

Natural Resource Data Series NPS/HTLN/NRDS—2012/270

Jennifer L. Haack

National Park Service
Heartland Network
6424 W Farm Road 182
Republic, MO 65738

March 2012

U.S. Department of the Interior
National Park Service
Natural Resource Stewardship and Science
Fort Collins, Colorado

The National Park Service, Natural Resource Stewardship and Science office in Fort Collins, Colorado publishes a range of reports that address natural resource topics of interest and applicability to a broad audience in the National Park Service and others in natural resource management, including scientists, conservation and environmental constituencies, and the public.

The Natural Resource Data Series is intended for the timely release of basic data sets and data summaries. Care has been taken to assure accuracy of raw data values, but a thorough analysis and interpretation of the data has not been completed. Consequently, the initial analyses of data in this report are provisional and subject to change.

All manuscripts in the series receive the appropriate level of peer review to ensure that the information is scientifically credible, technically accurate, appropriately written for the intended audience, and designed and published in a professional manner.

This report received informal peer review by subject-matter experts who were not directly involved in the collection, analysis, or reporting of the data.

Views, statements, findings, conclusions, recommendations, and data in this report do not necessarily reflect views and policies of the National Park Service, U.S. Department of the Interior. Mention of trade names or commercial products does not constitute endorsement or recommendation for use by the U.S. Government.

This report is available from http://science.nature.nps.gov/im/units/htln/articles.cfm and the Natural Resource Publications Management website http://www.nature.nps.gov/publications/nrpm/.

Please cite this publication as:

Haack, J. L. 2012. Thicket Monitoring at Homestead National Monument of America of 2000 - 2010. Natural Resource Data Series NPS/HTLN/NRDS—2012/270. National Park Service, Fort Collins, Colorado.

NPS 368/113322, March 2012

Contents

Figures

Tables

Appendices

Acknowledgments

I would like to acknowledge Jesse Bolli at Homestead NM of America for his help and input with this project. I would also like to thank Chad Gross and Brittany Cole for their help.

Introduction

Homestead National Monument of America (HOME) is located in the southeast corner of Nebraska (Figure 1). The Monument was established in 1936 to commemorate the Homestead Act of 1862, a law intended to stimulate the agricultural economy through free land deeds. HOME includes the 160 acres once owned by Daniel Freeman, who is credited with filing the first homestead claim in the United States (Hutchinson, 1992). For the settlers of the Great Plains, the prairie initially provided food for livestock and housing by way of sod. A great deal of original prairie has since been converted for agricultural purposes. In 1939 a hundred acres of land at HOME was restored to tallgrass prairie, making it the second oldest prairie restoration in the country. The restored prairie can provide a comprehensive historical view of what the landscape looked like at the time of the early settlers.

Prairies are unique plant communities containing a wealth of diversity in grass and forb species. This composition is a result from the influence of fire, intermittent heavy grazing, and cyclical droughts over thousands of years (Sutton et al., 1984). Often prairies are referred to as seas of grass, as the occurrence of fire and grazing kept the presence of woody species at a minimum. As the prairies became settled, wildfires were intentionally suppressed and woody species began invading the prairie land. Although the presence of a few small thickets is important for animal life and providing food and shelter, an expansive thicket population can be detrimental to prairie existence. Thus, a management goal for HOME is to reduce thicket presence to a manageable 15% of the prairie.

To assist in decisions regarding thicket management, a mapping project was conducted in the restored tallgrass prairie of HOME in the summer of 2000. Additional thicket mapping was done in 2001 in conjunction with treatment efforts. Thicket mapping was continued every five years, allowing for a long term view of the success of management practices in reducing thicket colonies. Thickets were mapped in 2005 and again in 2010. The primary objective of the thicket mapping project is to determine the total area occupied by woody shrub species in the restored prairie.

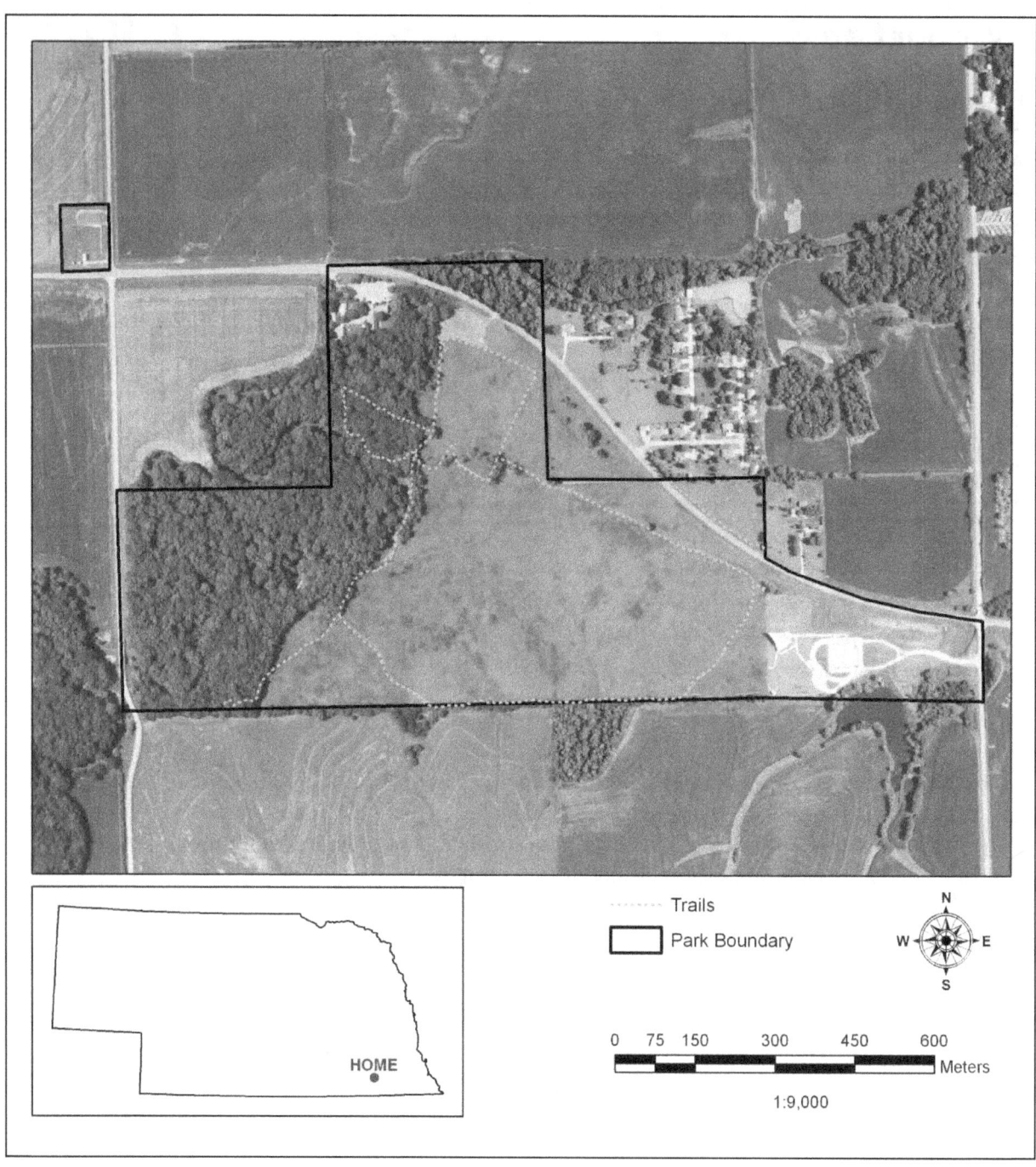

Figure 1. Map of Homestead National Monument of America.

Methods

Thicket monitoring at HOME, which started in 2000, took place every five years during the growing season. All woody thickets within the 98 acre prairie of HOME were spatially documented with a GPS unit. For this study Trimble GPS units with TerraSync Professional software were used. The GPS models used for each year were the ProXR in 2000, GeoExplorer 3 in 2005, and GeoXT & GeoXH in 2010. All thickets were collected as polygons features with a 1 second logging interval with the projection of UTM North America 1983 CONUS CORS96, zone 14 North. For this study the definition of a thicket is a patch of small trees or shrubs present in the prairie area. Older trees, such as the mulberries/cottonwoods present by the trail and the Osage orange hedgerow, are excluded from being considered a thicket.

Along with each thickets' location the dominant species type and density category were recorded. The species present at HOME over the last decade are *Cornus* spp. (dogwood), *Fraxinus* spp. (ash), *Gleditsia* spp. (honeylocust), *Prunus* spp. (plum/cherry), *Rhus* spp. (sumac), and *Sambucus* spp. (elderberry). The density categories ranging from 1 to 4 are listed below with their definition. After the thickets were collected the software Pathfinder Office was used to download the rover files, differentially correct, and export the data into shapefiles for analysis.

Density Categories

Category 1
Area of dense thickets with warm season grasses (e.g. big blue, switch, Indian, little blue) absent or nearly so. Warm season grasses persisting only along thicket perimeter. Forbs few, less than 25% foliar cover. Shrub cover greater than 75%.

Characteristic species found in the understory of dense shrubs in the upper prairie: *Ambrosia artemisifolia* (ragweed), *Solidago* spp (goldenrod), *Oxalis* spp (sorrel), *Cameacrist fasciculata* (partridge pea), *Verbena urticifolia* (vervain), *Mirabilis nyctaginaceae* (four-o'-clock).

Characteristic species found in the understory of dense shrubs in the lower prairie: *Poa pratense* (poa), *Apocynum canabinum* (dogbane), *Solidago* spp (goldenrod), *Verbena urticifolia* (vervain), *Muhlenbergia racemosa* (muhly), *Polygonum pennsylvanica* (pinkweed).

Category 2
Area primarily of dense thickets with some space among thickets occupied by tallgrass prairie interspersed with woody stems.

Category 3
Area primarily of tallgrass prairie interspersed with woody stems with occasional patches of dense thickets.

Category 4
Area of typical tallgrass prairie grasses and forbs with woody stems interspersed. Dense patches of thickets absent. Woody shrub cover 40% – 60%, warm season grass cover greater than 75%.

Results

In 2010, 28.3 acres of thickets were mapped (Figure 2). The area of thickets in 2010 is the highest observed over the decade of monitoring and represents an increase in 7 acres from 2005 (Figure 3), and an overall 5 acre increase since 2000 (Figure 4). Plum thickets declined by approximately 4 acres between 2000 and 2005, and remained sparse between 2005 and 2010 (Table 1, Figure 5). On the other hand, sumac originally declined from 11.6 to 8.5 acres between 2005 and 2010, but rebounded to a total area of 16.1 acres in 2010 (Table 1, Figure 5). The area of dogwood thickets increased nearly 50% over the 10 year period to 10.6 acres (Table 1, Figure 5). Sumac and dogwood account for the majority of the increased area of thickets observed in 2010. A new population of honeylocust was discovered in 2010 and the ash thicket was completed removed between 2005 and 2010 (Table 1 and Figure 5). The small populations of elderberry that were noted in the 2000 and 2005 surveys were no longer visible or grouped in with a larger thicket during the 2010 survey.

The largest and most dense thickets, however, are decreasing in area. The total area assigned a density category of one (i.e. the most dense) decreased from 5.9 acres in 2000 to 2.3 acres in 2010 (Figure 6). The largest reductions were seen with sumac (2.2 acres in 2000 to 0.4 acres in 2010) and the complete removal of the approximately 1 acre ash thicket (Table 1, Figure 5). Over the same period, the average polygon size of areas mapped as category 1 decreased from 0.26 acres to 0.06 acres, and the number of dense thickets greater than 0.25 acres in size decreased from 6 in 2000 to 2 in 2010 (Table 2).

Table 1. Thicket area in acres for species and density categories.

Species by year	Density Category (1,2,3,4)				Total Acres
2010	1	2	3	4	Σ
Dogwood	1.668	2.764	4.331	1.854	10.617
Ash	0	0	0	0	0
Honeylocust	0	0	0	0.003	0.003
Plum	0.176	0.435	0.841	0.090	1.543
Sumac	0.436	7.889	6.370	1.457	16.152
Elderberry	0	0	0	0	0
2010 Totals	2.280	11.088	11.542	3.404	**28.315**
2005	1	2	3	4	Σ
Dogwood	1.700	5.103	2.538	0.471	9.812
Ash	0.916	0	0	0.129	1.045
Honeylocust	0	0	0	0	0
Plum	0.476	0.110	0.701	0.204	1.491
Sumac	1.601	2.431	2.301	2.140	8.473
Elderberry	0.058	0.196	0.037	0	0.291
2005 Totals	4.752	7.841	5.576	2.945	**21.114**
2000	1	2	3	4	Σ
Dogwood	1.988	0.573	0.950	1.709	5.221
Ash	0.970	0	0	0	0.970
Honeylocust	0	0	0	0	0
Plum	0.635	2.366	1.126	1.202	5.328
Sumac	2.210	2.278	1.937	5.195	11.621
Elderberry	0.075	0	0	0	0.075
2000 Totals	5.879	5.217	4.013	8.106	**23.215**

Table 2. Total area, average map unit size, and total number of map units greater than 0.25 acres assigned to density category one.

	2010	2005	2000
Total area (acres) assigned a density category of one (i.e. most dense)	2.3	4.8	5.9
Average size (acres) of polygons assigned to density category one (i.e. most dense)	0.06	0.11	0.26
Number of polygons greater than 0.25 acres assigned a density category of one (i.e. most dense)	2	3	6

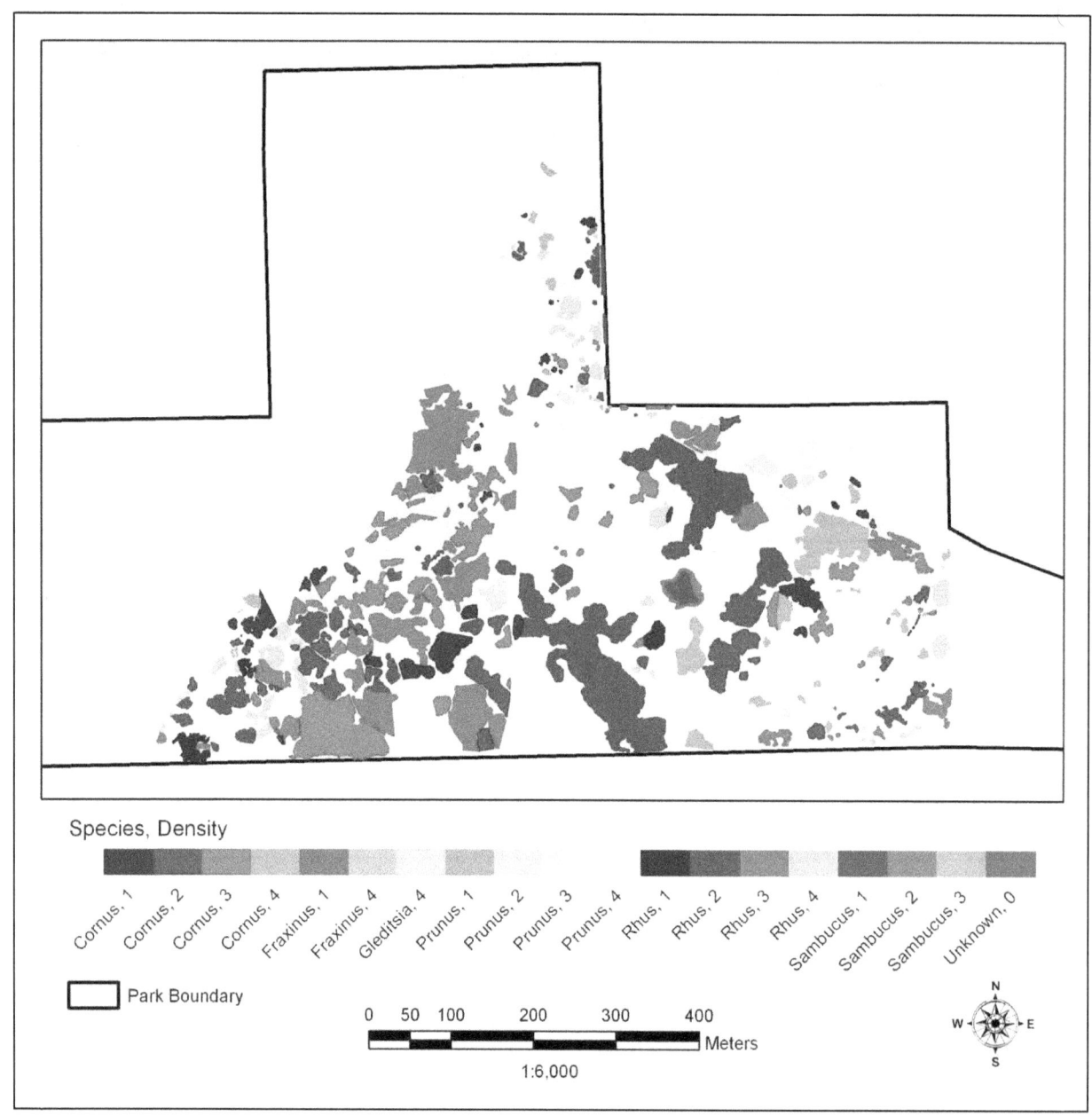

Figure 2. Map of 2010 thicket locations at Homestead National Monument of America.

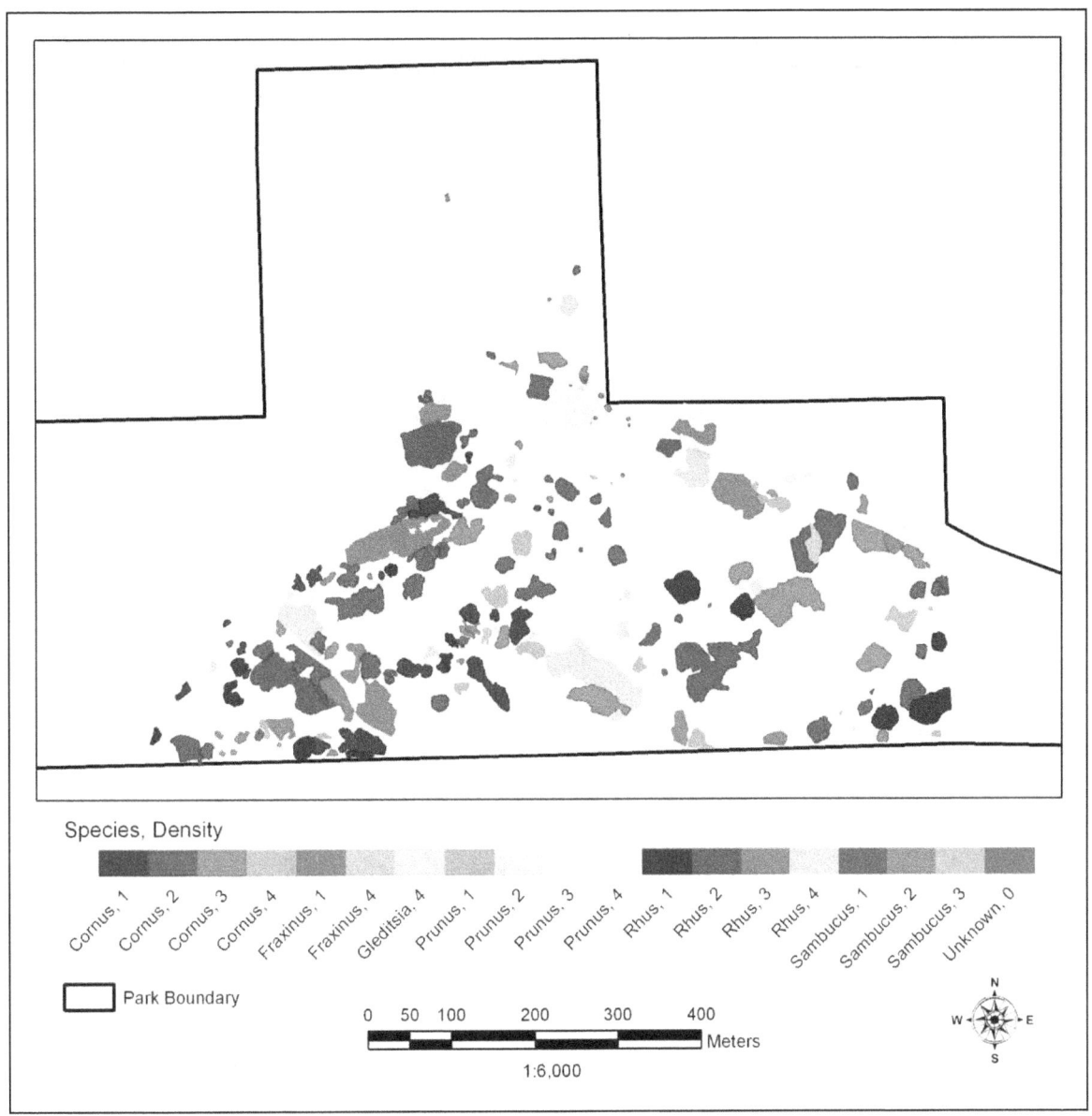

Figure 3. Map of 2005 thicket locations at Homestead National Monument of America.

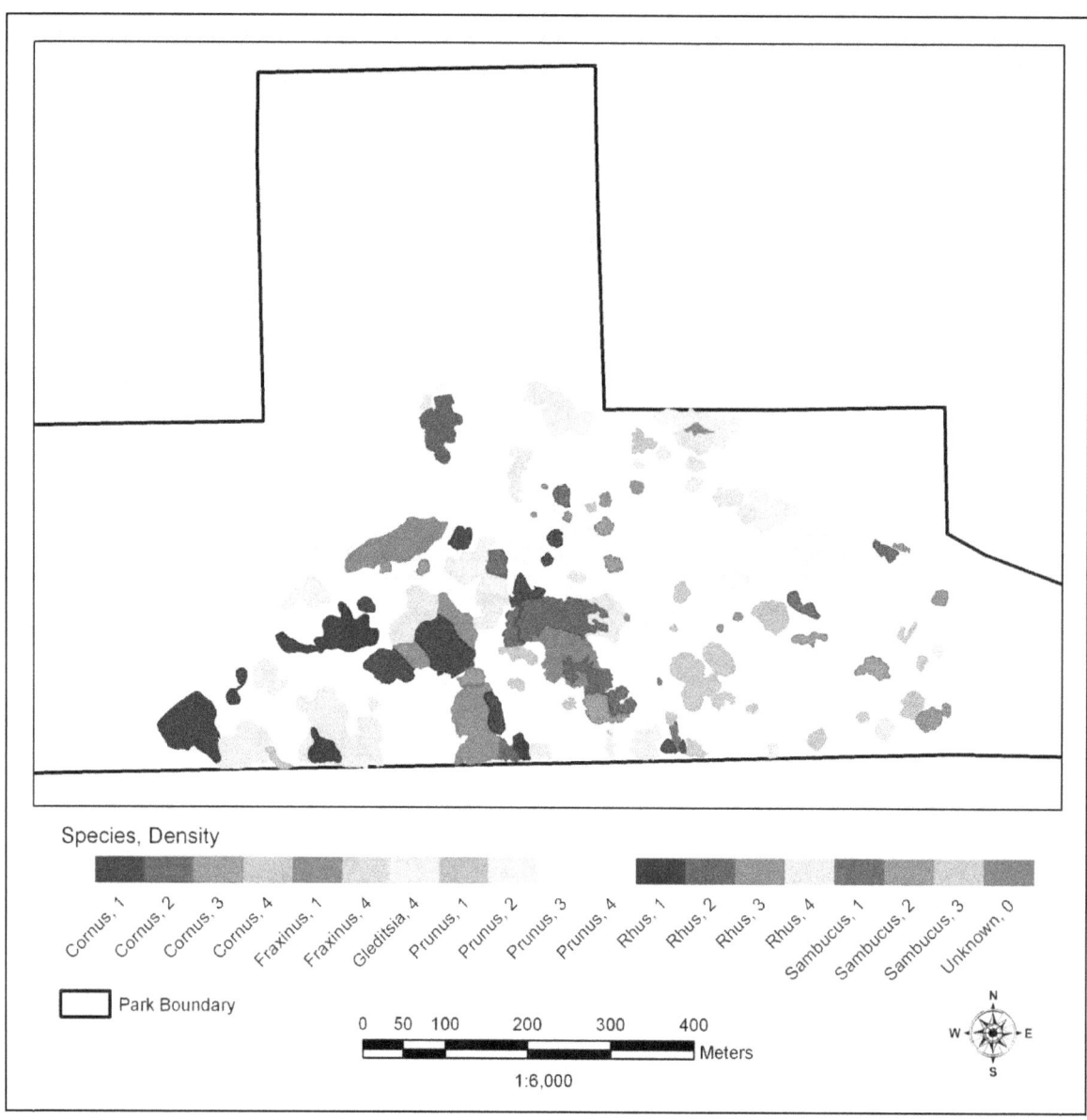

Figure 4. Map of 2000 thicket locations at Homestead National Monument of America.

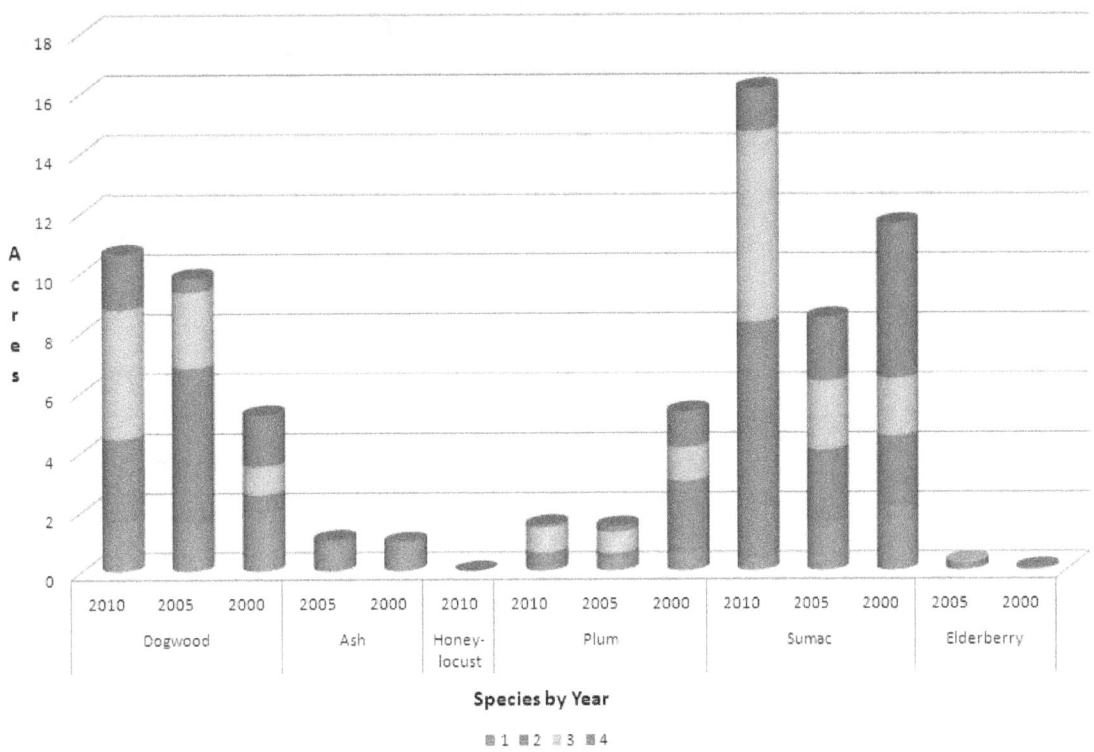

Figure 5. Graph of thicket acres per density category for each year. Y-axis is amount of acres, while X-axis shows species present by sample year. The colors indicate density categories.

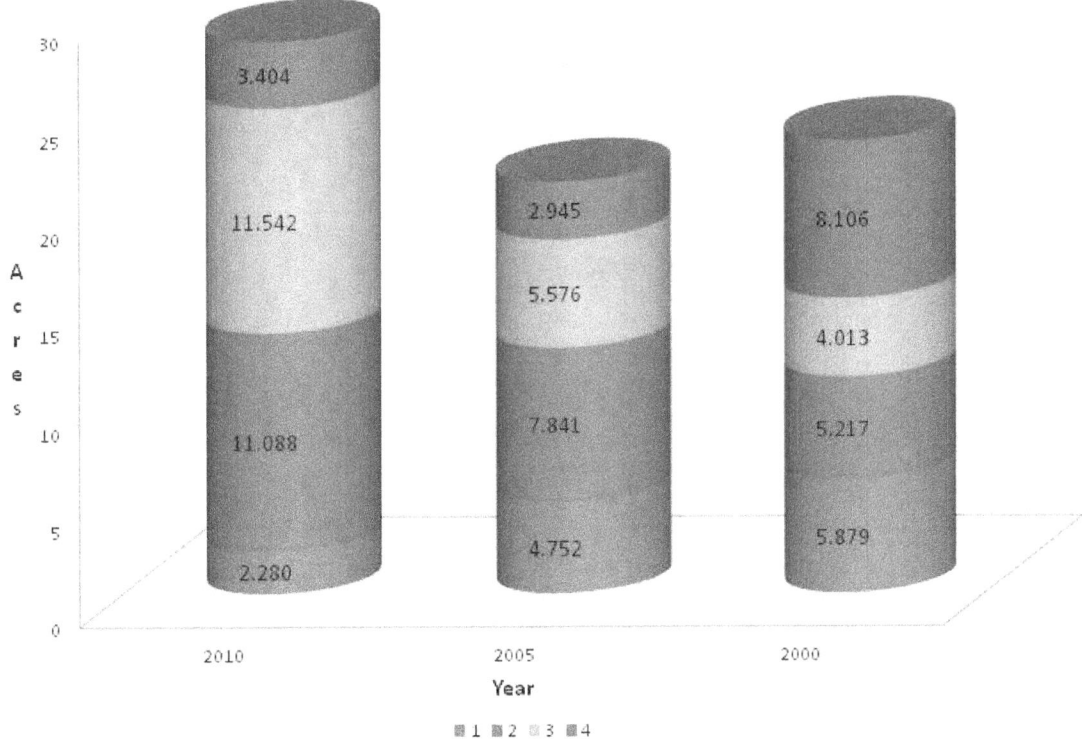

Figure 6. Graph representing thicket density categories per year. The colors indicate density categories.

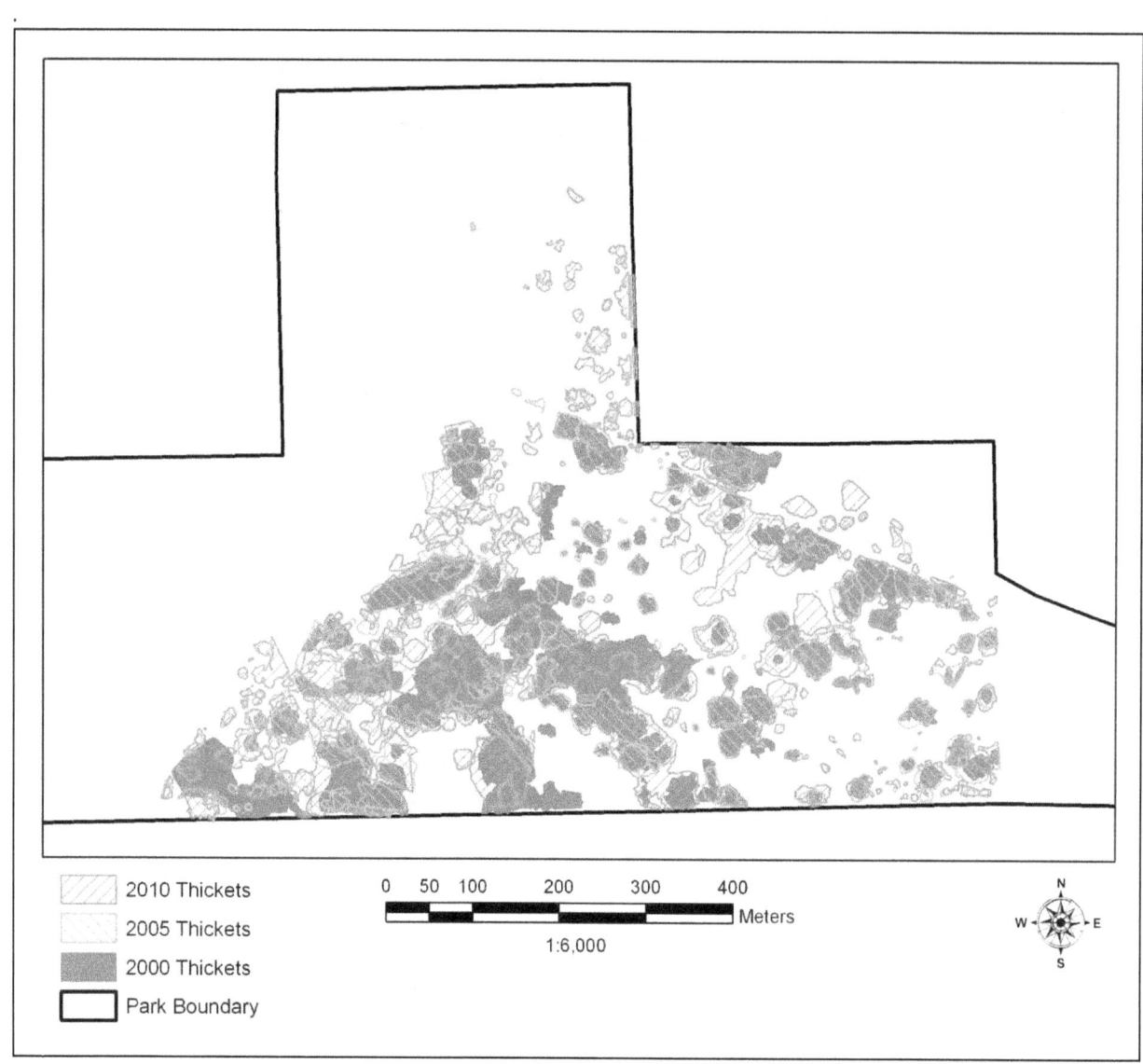

Figure 7. Map of all three years of thicket surveys.

Discussion

The Vegetation Management Action Plan 2004-2014 (NPS 2006) prescribes actions to limit the extent of thickets in the HOME prairie to no more than 15% of the gross area, or roughly 15 acres. The plan further states that dense thickets (i.e. category 1) occupy no more than 5% of the gross area. One strategy to achieve these goals is to shrink the size of the largest and most dense thickets so that no thickets assigned a density category 1 are greater than 0.25 acres in size. Twenty-eight acres of shrubs were mapped in 2010 exceeding the goal by over 13 acres. However, only 2.3 acres of dense thickets were mapped in 2010, representing a 50% reduction since 2000. Management actions have also been effective in reducing the size of the largest and most dense thickets. The number of dense thickets exceeding 0.25 acres in size decreased from 6 in 2000 to 2 in 2010.

Control of thickets in the HOME prairie requires persistence and a variety of approaches, tools and resources. Appendix A lists the management practices used to control the invasion of woody thickets over the last decade. Anecdotal observations suggest undesirable species like smooth brome may be colonizing treated areas, and that some treatments may only achieve short term results. For example, dogwood was seen vigorously re-sprouting in areas that were cut the previous year (Bolli 2005). Re-vegetation may be required in areas where prairie plants have been completed shaded out by dense thickets.

Prescribed fire is an important prairie management tool. Currently the prairie is burned on a three year rotation for the purposes of reducing thickets and cool-season grasses, and to stimulate growth of warm season, prairie grasses. A 15-year study at Konza biological station using spring fires revealed that shrubs were best controlled with annual fire. Intermediate fire frequency (every four years) increased densities over both low frequency (every 20 years) and annual burning (Briggs et al. 2002b).

Sumac is highly fire tolerant and spreads through rhizomes, lateral roots with vertical roots extending at each node. This growth form allows sumac to resprout quickly following disturbance. Mowing and fire appear most effective in controlling sumac when conducted following flowering. Disturbance prior to the growing season (i.e. winter/early spring) result in an increase in stem density rather than a reduction (Aldous 1934; Adams et al. 1982). Similarly, dogwoods have the ability to resprout and exhibit high tolerance to fire. Managers may consider an annual or biennial fire return interval to improve thicket control.

Thicket control may become even more problematic in the future as it has been suggested that increased CO^2 in the atmosphere favors woody plants. Carbon and nitrogen enrichment from the air and precipitation may present favorable conditions for the spread of thickets in grasslands (Harmens et al. 2004, Springsteen et al. 2010).

Park managers intensified thicket control efforts in 2011 (see appendix A, Figure 18). New techniques using triclopyr in basal bark applications, and an herbicide applicator wick allowed crews to treat larger areas more efficiently with glyphosate. Preliminary data and observations indicate these efforts were successful in reducing the extent or thickets in the prairie (NPS unpulished data, Jesse Bolli, personal communication).

11

Literature Cited

Aldous, A.E. 1934. Effect of burning on Kansas bluestem pastures. Kansas technical bulletin 38:3-64.

Adams, D.E.; R.C. Anderson; and S.L. Collins. 1982. Differential response of woody and herbaceous species to summer and winter burning in an Oklahoma grassland. The Southwest Naturalist. 27: 55-61

Bolli, Jesse. 2005. Unpublished document concerning management actions with regard to thickets 2001 – 2005. NPS.

Bolli, Jesse. 2012. Unpublished document listing the 2005 – 2010 thicket management actions. NPS.

Briggs, J.M., A.K. Knapp, and B.L. Brock. 2002. Expansion of woody plants in tallgrass prairie: a fifteen-year study of fire and fire-grazing interactions. American Midland Naturalist 147:287-294

Harmens H., P. D. Williams, S. L. Peters, M. T. Bambrick, A. Hopkins, and T. W. Ashenden. 2004. Impacts of elevated atmospheric CO_2 and temperature on plant community structure of a temperate grassland are modulated by cutting frequency. Grass and Forage Science 59:144-156.

Hutchinson, D. E. 1992. Restoration of the Tall Grass Prairie at Homestead National Monument, Beatrice, Nebraska. Ranglands 14(3):174-175

Springsteen, A., W. Loya, M. Liebig, and J. Hendrickson. 2010. Soil carbon and nitrogen across a chronosequence of woody plant expansion in North Dakota. Plant and Soil 328: 369-379.

Sutton Richard K., James Stubbendieck, and Jayne Traeger. 1984. Vegetation Survey and Management Recommendations: Homestead National Monument of America. Natural Resources Enterprises, Inc., Lincoln, Nebraska.

National Park Service. 2006. Homestead National Monument of America Vegetation Management Action Plan 2004 – 2014. NPS.

Appendices
Appendix A: Treatment History

Below is a list of the actions as reported in the HOME Prairie Management Action Log that are targeted towards thicket management. The Logs are to be completed for each project that impacts the prairie vegetation (Bolli 2005 & 2012).

2001 (See Figure 9)
- On 5/18/2001, the middle third of the prairie was treated with prescribed fire (~35 acres).
- Cut 300 *Sumac spp.* in Pioneer Acres.
- Cut *Sumac spp.* with brush hog near weather station, some was sprayed with Garlon 3A.
- Brushhogged plum near highway in East 40.
- Cut trees and thicket in farm loop.
- Cut plum etc. near boardwalk.
- Cut plum near creek with sickle bar mower.
- Pioneer Acres triangle was hayed.

2002 (See Figure 10)
- On 5/31/2002, the upper third of the prairie was treated with prescribed fire (~27 acres).
- Cut *Sumac spp.*, *Cornus spp.* (Dogwood), and *Morrus spp.* (Mulberry) near NE corner of farm loop trail.
- Stump treated some of the thickets; cut bigger ones with chainsaw.
- In August, used brushhog to cut large areas of thickets within the upland loop trails; did note the following year that smooth brome was invading these areas.
- Pioneer Acres triangle was hayed in August.

2003 (See Figure 11)
- On 5/12/2003, the lower third of the prairie was treated with prescribed fire (~39 acres).
- Hand cut *Sumac spp.* and *Cornus spp.* (Dogwood) East 40 stump treated approximately 2 acres.
- Hand cut clearing the state triangle and areas along trail.
- Cut brush around first cabin site.
- Cut brush in East 40.
- Pioneer Acres triangle was hayed in August.

2004 (See Figure 12)
- Cut dogwood in east forty 65 hrs used mainly weed wrenches, treated only trees with Garlon 3A.

2005 (See Figure 13)
- Approximately 19 acres of prairie was managed for woody species. Treatment mainly consisted of cutting *Cornus spp.* (Dogwood) and *Rhus spp.* (Sumac) mostly in area near ash thicket with lopper and treating 4.7 acres of cut trees with Garlon.
- Pioneer Acres triangle was hayed in August.
- On 9/15/2005, about 30 acres in the middle prairie was treated with prescribed fire.

2006
- Five acres of thickets were mowed down by using a tractor and rotary mower.
- Approximately one acre of thickets were hand cut and stump treated with Garlon 3A.
- Approximately 100 trees within the prairie were cut and treated with a chemical.
- On 10/6/2006 about 23 acres of the eastern prairie was treated with prescribed fire.

2007
- Approximately two acres of *Cornus spp.* (Dogwood) was treated with chemical in early August.
- On 9/11/2007, about 24 acres in the western prairie was treated with prescribed fire.

2008 (See Figure 14)
- Approximately four acres of thickets were treated with Garlon 3A.
- Approximately six acres were mowed with a rotary mower.
- Approximately 0.25 acre of thickets were manually cut and stump treated
- On 4/28/2008, about 25 acres of prairie was treated with prescribed fire (unit 4 and part of unit 1).

2009 (See Figure 15)
- Approximately 95% of the *Fraxinus spp.* (Ash) thicket was felled and treated with herbicide.
- 9.7 acres of thickets were treated with Element 3A.
- On 5/6/2009, about 39 acres of prairie in units 2 and 3 were treated with prescribed fire.

2010 (See Figure 16)
- The remaining 5% (0.07 acre) of the *Fraxinus spp.* (Ash) thicket was downed.
- Before July 2010 mapping: Mowed fire line
- Note: all remaining 2010 treatment was conducted after the thickets were mapped
    - In September 2010, 14.519 acres of thickets were treated: 1.579 acres were hand cut with loppers and stump treated with 100% Garlon 3A, 4.85 acres were mowed with a brush hog, and 8.09 acres were treated with herbicide by using a weed wick.
    - 27 acres were burned on 10/20/2010 (unit 1 and part or unit 2 and 4).

2011 (See Figure 17)

- April 2011: Manual and Triclopyr treatments
- June 2011: Triclopyr treatment
- September 2011: Prescribed burn of 23 acres
- November 2011: Basal Bark, Triclopyr, and Cut/Spray treatments

Appendix B: Treatment Maps

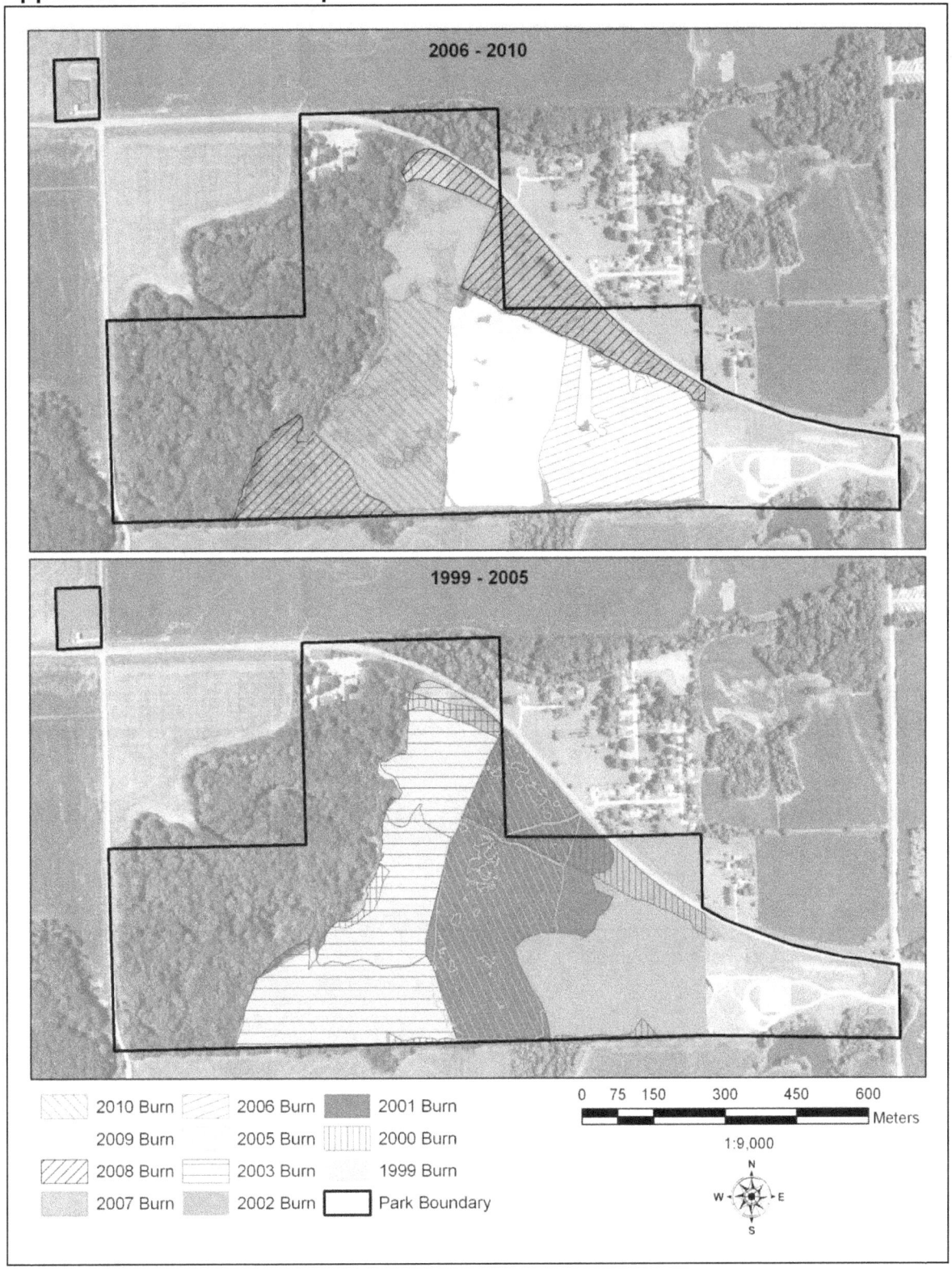

Figure 8. Map of 1999 -2010 burn areas at Homestead National Monument of America.

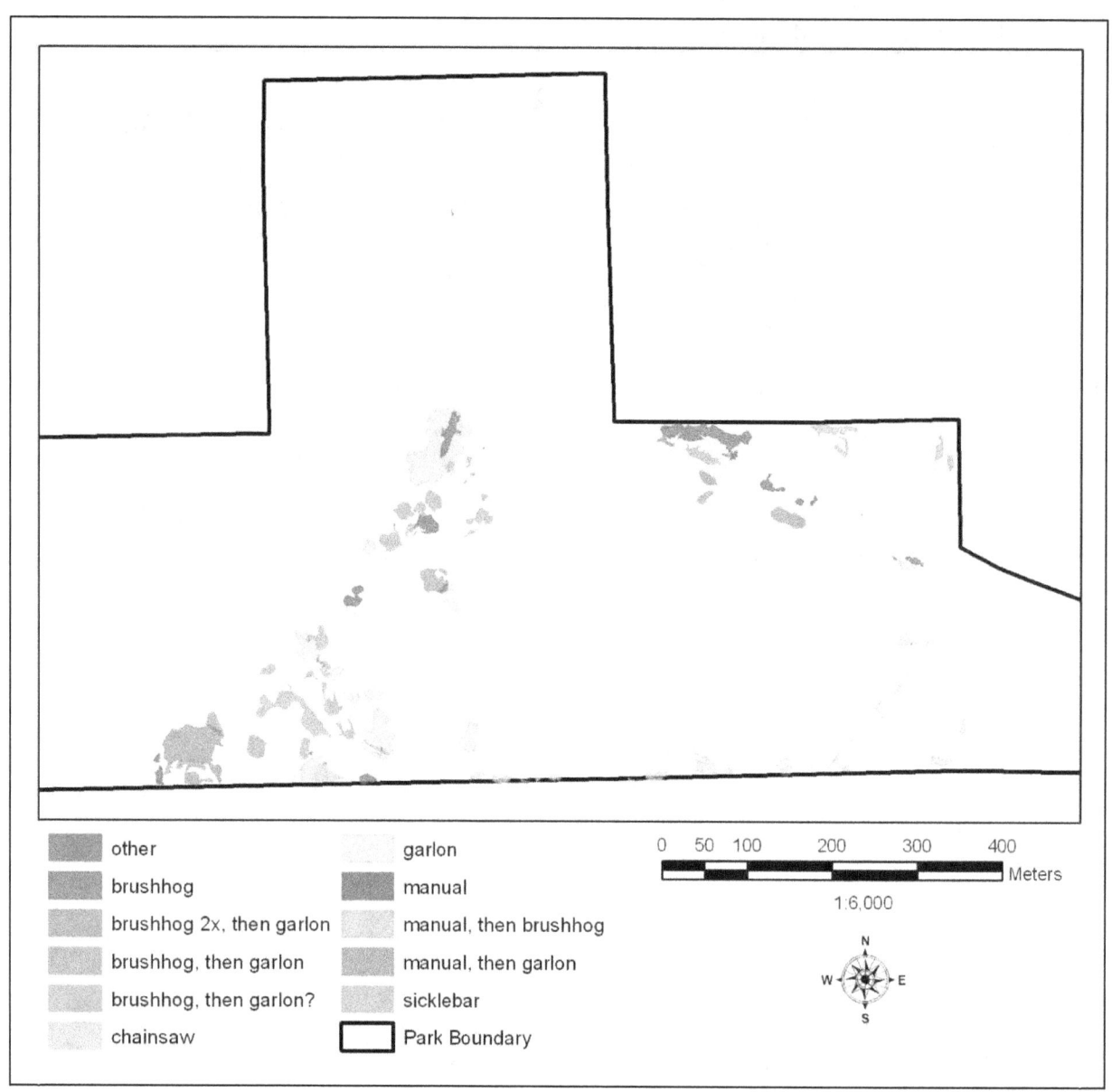

Figure 9. Map of 2001 thicket management.

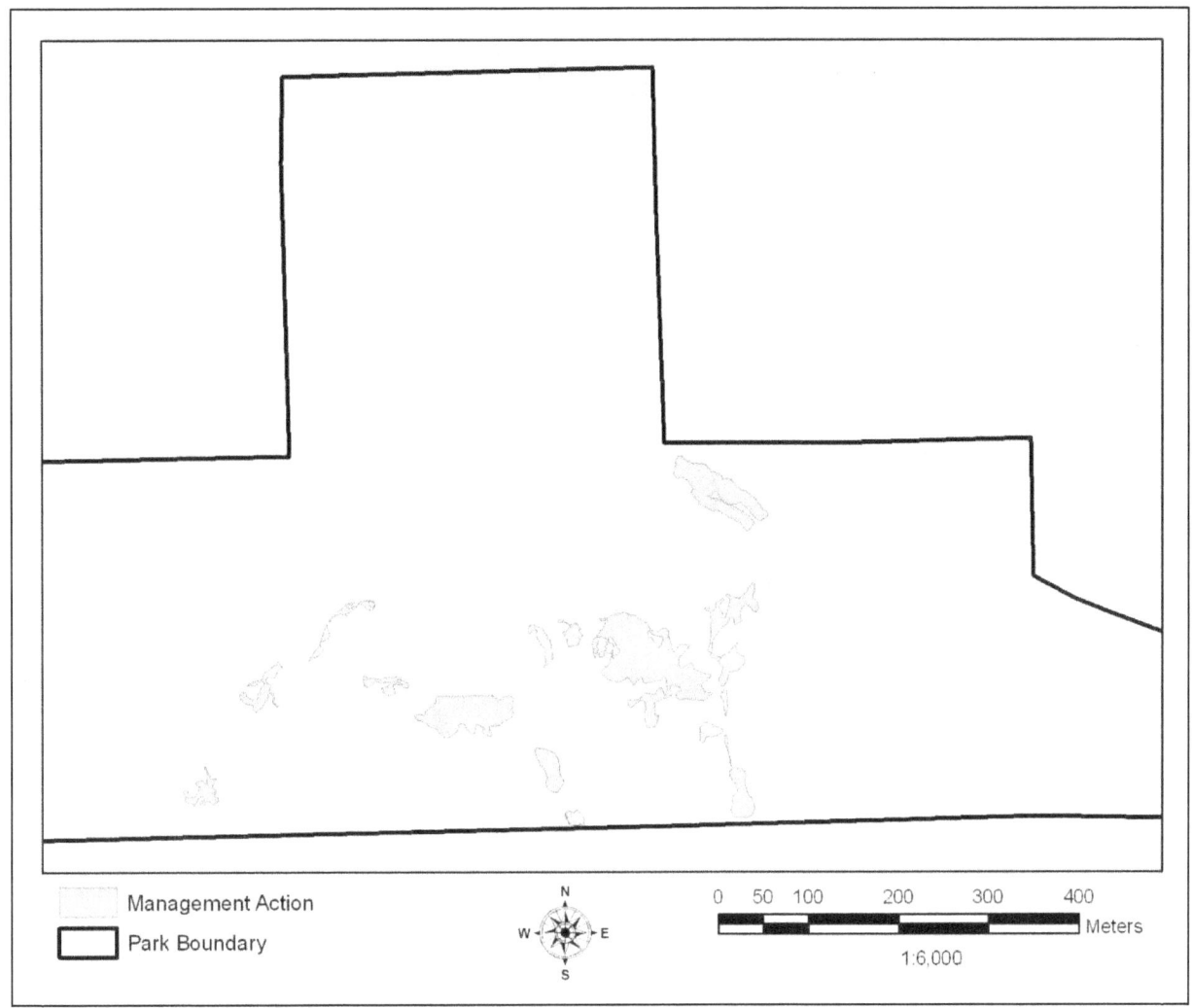

Figure 10. Map of 2002 thicket management.

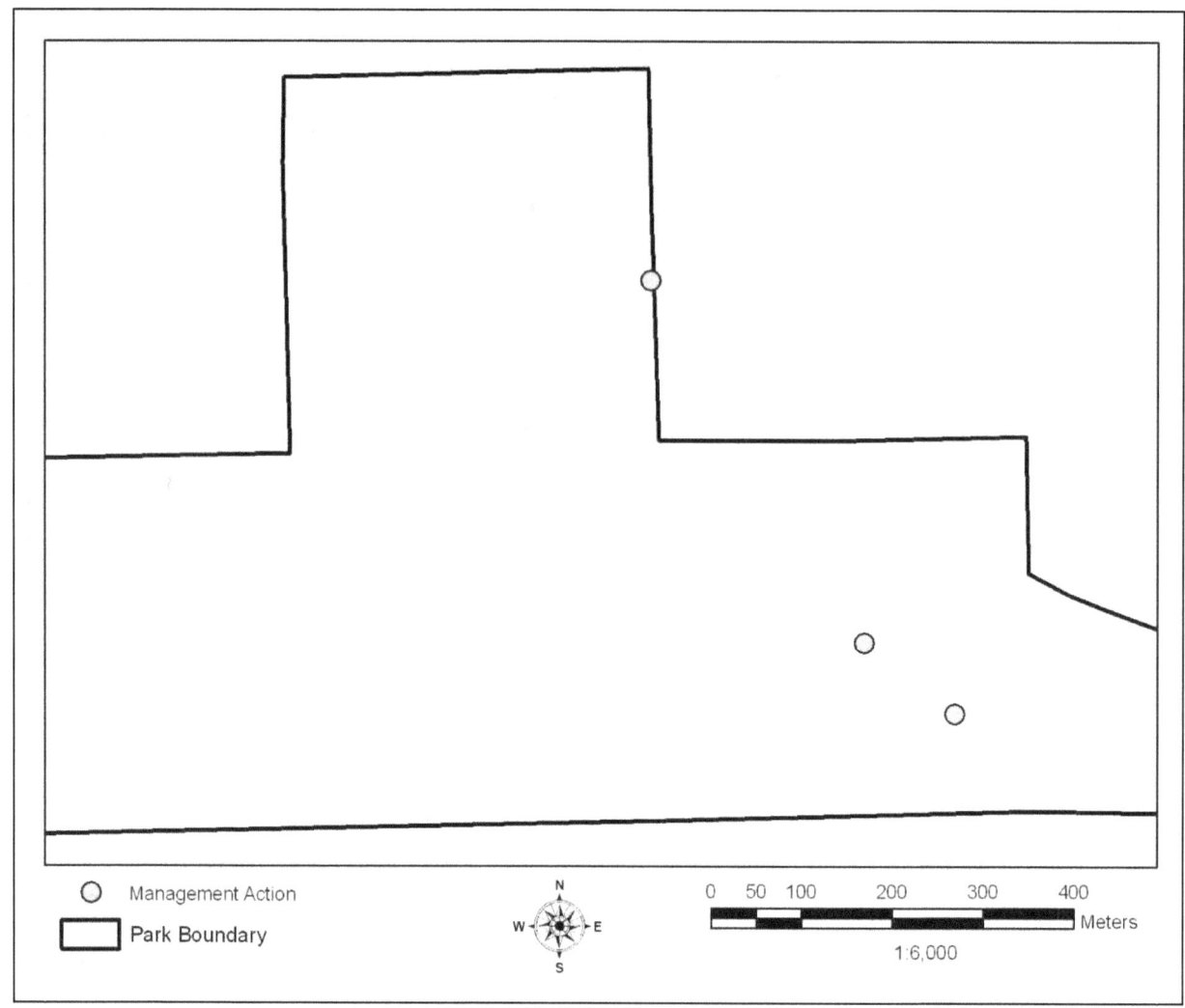

Figure 11. Map of 2003 thicket management.

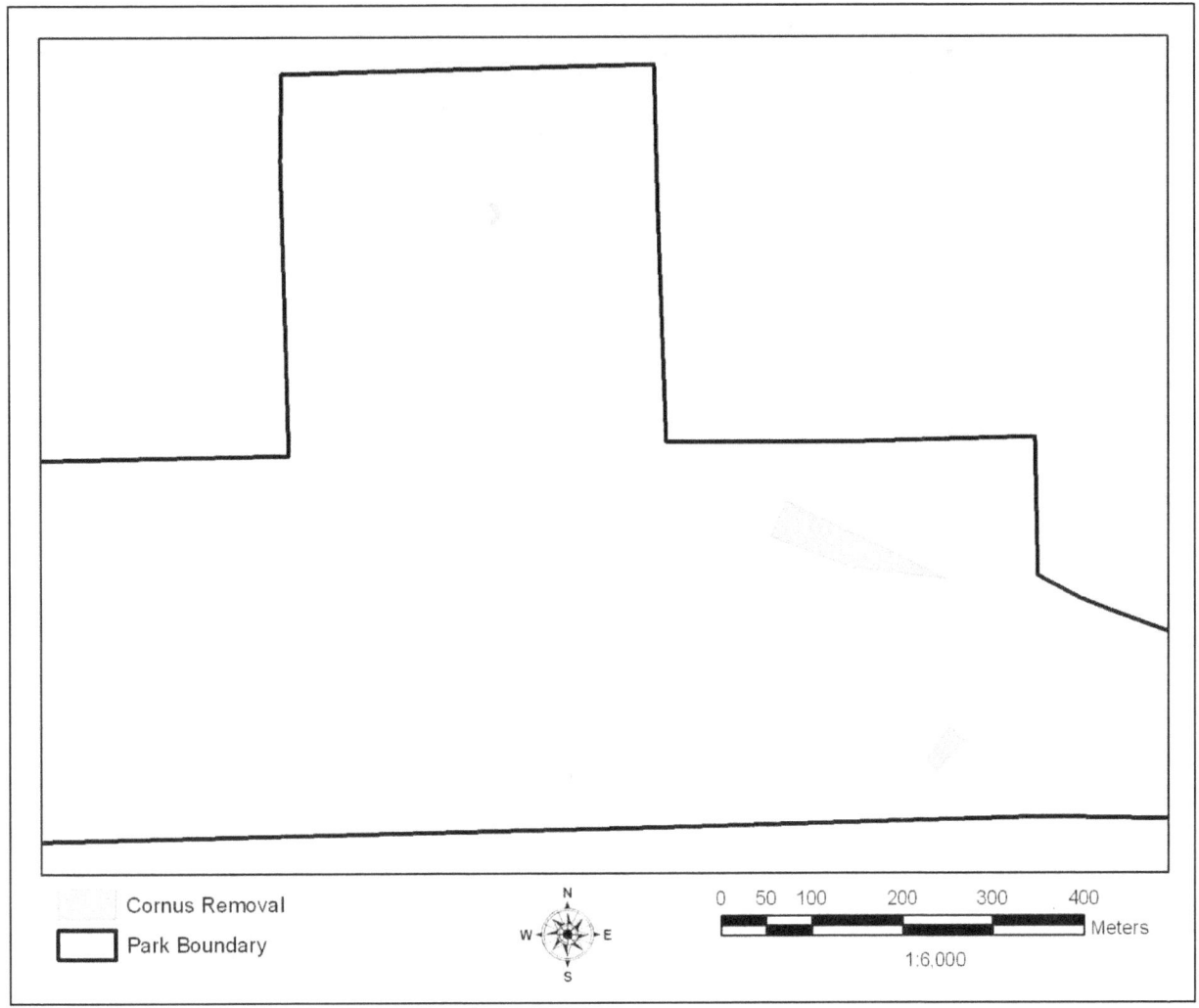

Figure 12. Map of 2004 thicket management.

Figure 13. Map of 2005 thicket management.

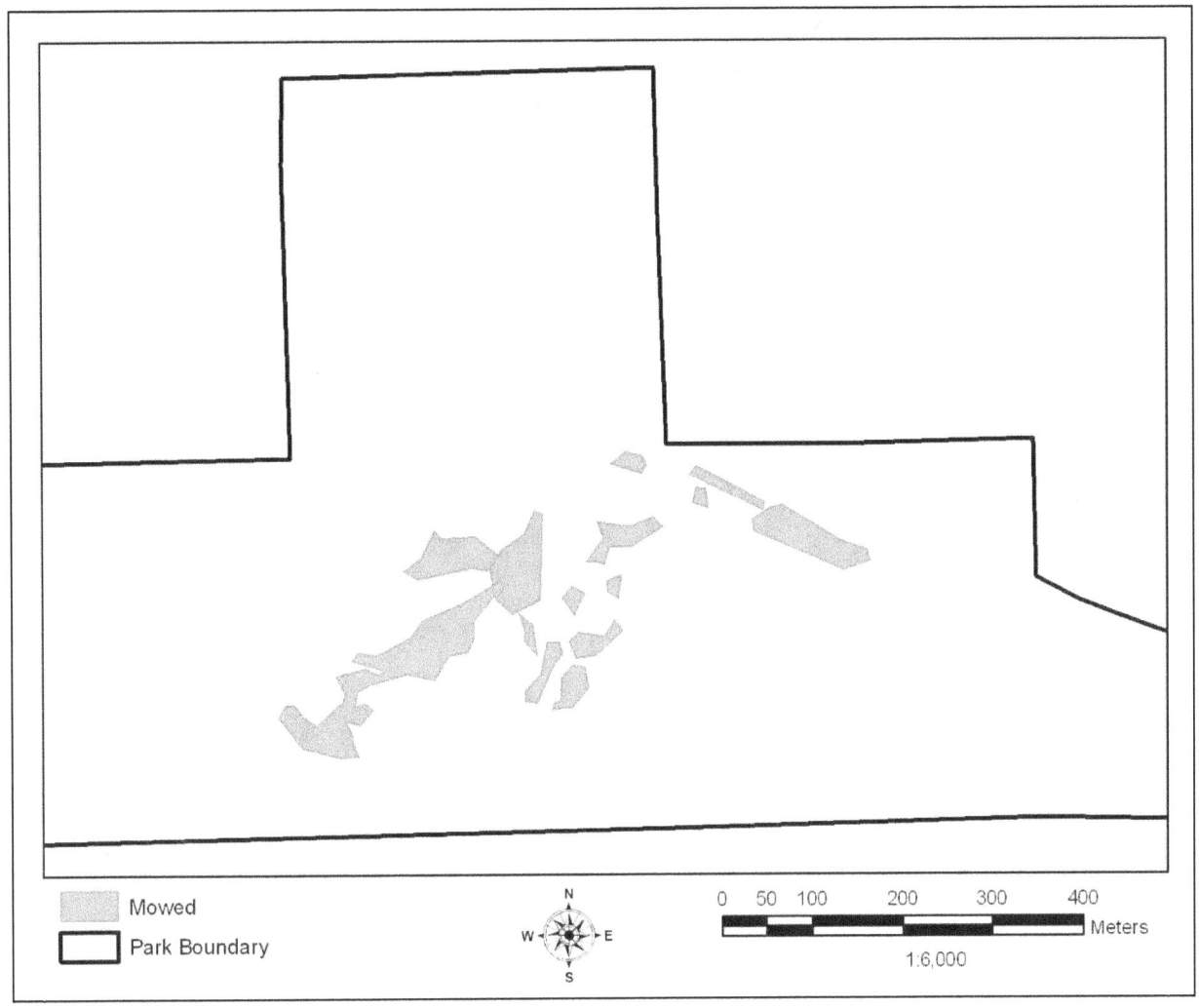

Figure 14. Map of 2008 thicket management.

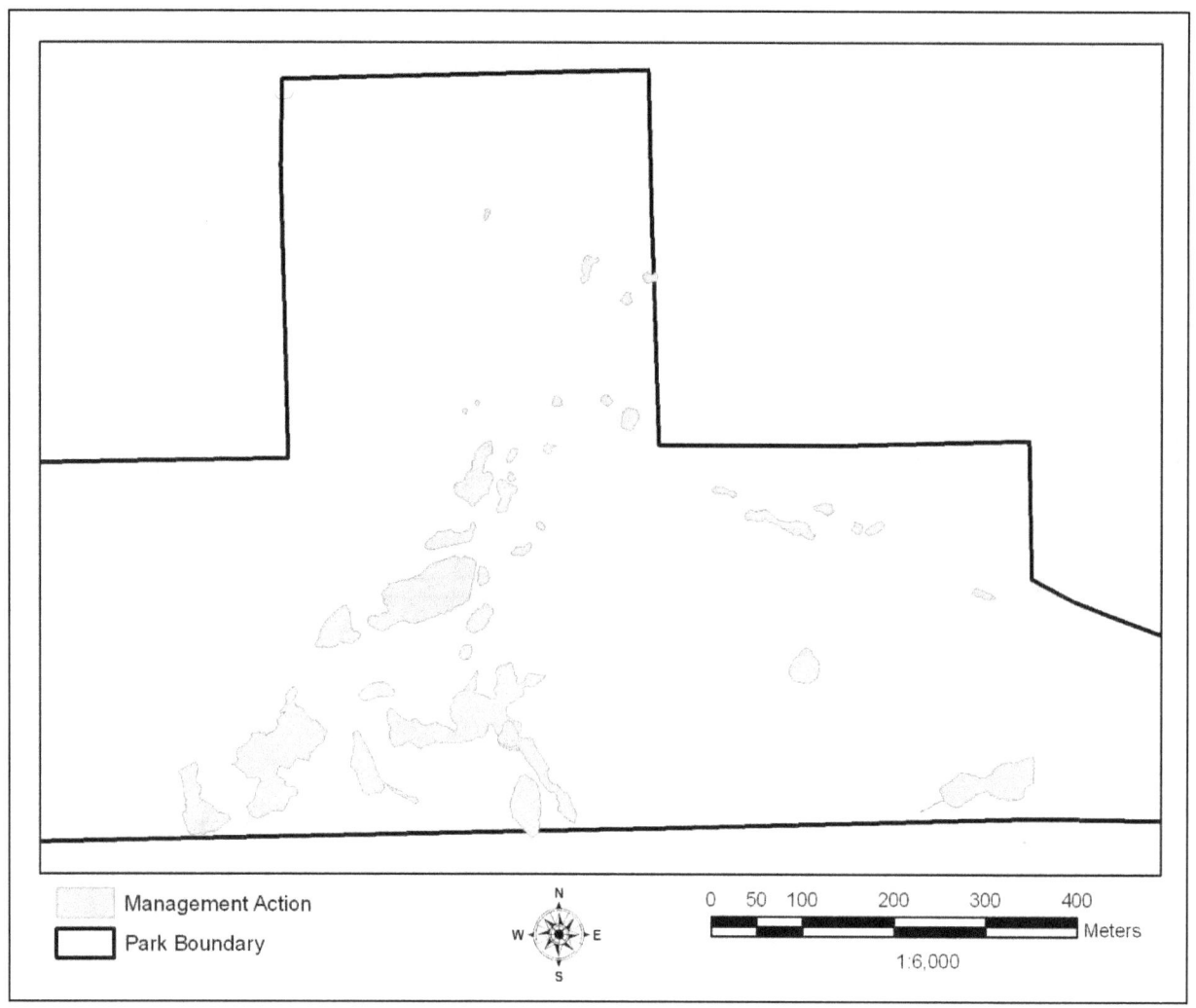

Figure 15. Map of 2009 thicket management.

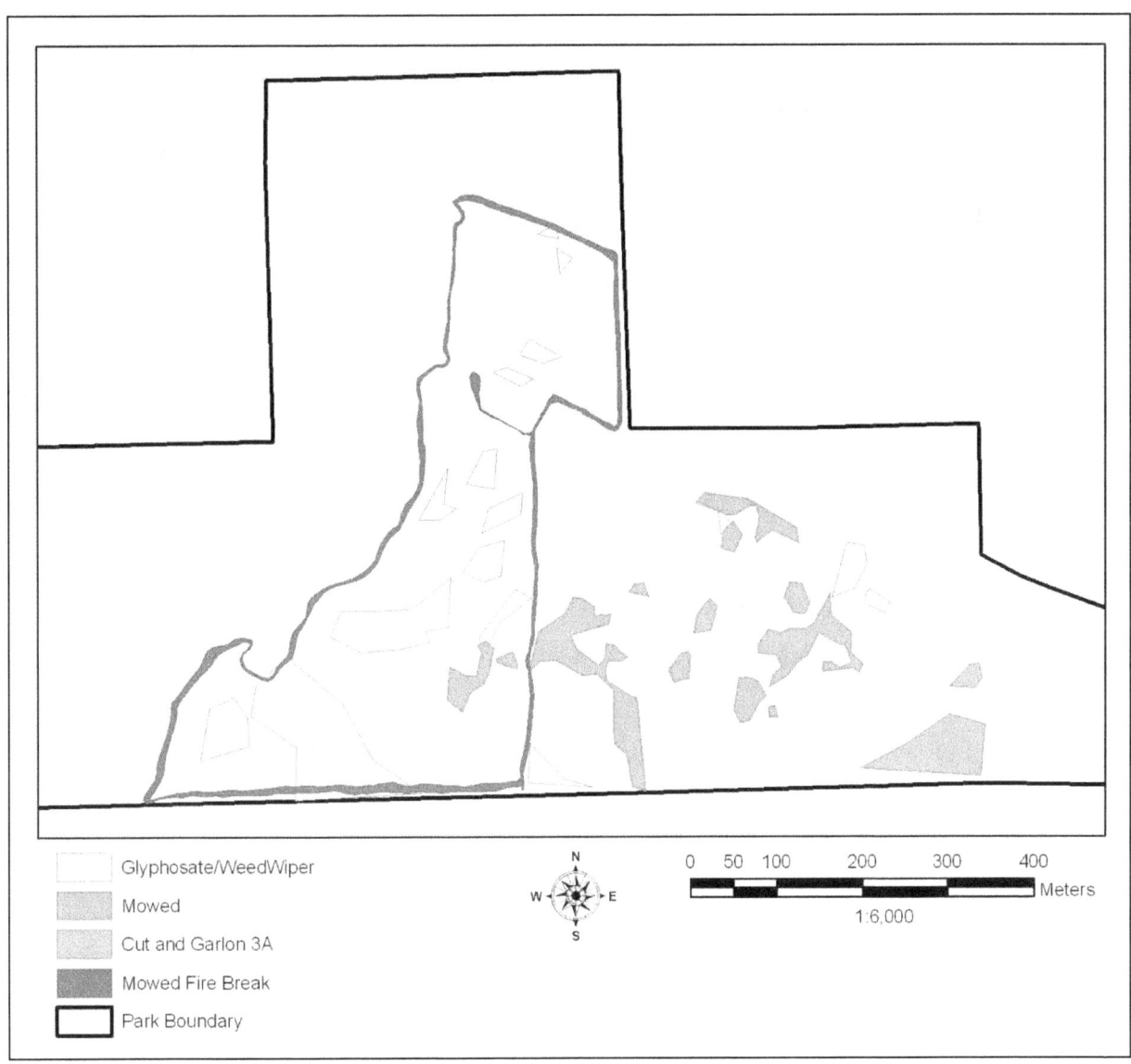

Figure 16. Map of 2010 thicket management.

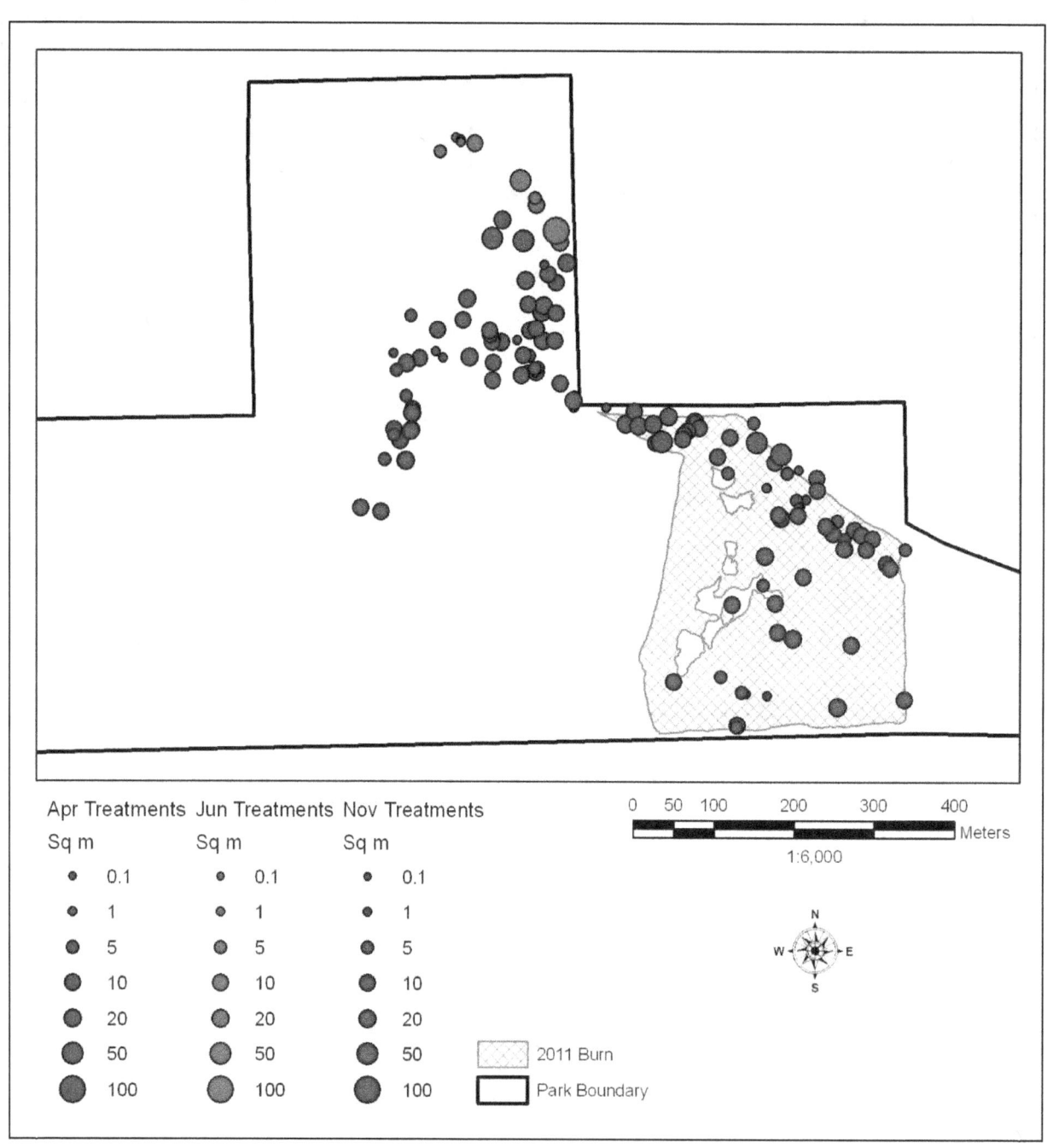

Figure 17. Map of 2011 thicket management.